T0208130

Zen Words for the Heart

Self-Portrait by Hakuin

Zen Words
for the Heart

Hakuin's Commentary on *The Heart Sutra*

Translated by Norman Waddell

Shambhala
Boston & London
1996

Shambhala Publications, Inc.
Horticultural Hall
300 Massachusetts Avenue
Boston, Massachusetts 02115
www.shambhala.com

Printed in the United States of America

Distributed in the United States by Random House, Inc.,
and in Canada by Random House of Canada Ltd

LIBRARY OF CONGRESS CATALOGING-IN-PUBLICATION DATA

Hakuin, 1686–1769
    [Hannya shingyō dokugochū. English]
    Zen words for the Heart: Hakuin's commentary on the Heart Sutra/translated by Norman Waddell.
        p.   cm.
    ISBN 1-57062-165-9 (alk. paper)
    1. Tripiṭaka. Sūtrapiṭaka. Prajñāpāramitā. Hṛdaya—Commentaries.
    I. Title.
BQ1965.H3413   1996   95-43420
294.3'85—dc20   CIP
BVG 01

For Yoshie

Contents

Translator's Introduction

The Sacred Tortoise's tail sweeps her
tracks clear. But how can the tail avoid
leaving traces of its own?

Zen Words for the Heart (*Dokugo shingyō* in Japanese) is a commentary on the *Heart Sutra* by the Japanese monk Hakuin Ekaku, 1686–1768. It brings together one of the great masters of Zen history and a scripture many rank among the most sublime documents of the human spirit.

Hakuin's commentary derives in large part, if not entirely, from lectures he delivered on the *Heart Sutra* at a practice meeting held in the winter of 1744 at a country temple in the province of Kai (present-day Yamanashi prefecture), near Mount Fuji.* He was, at the age of sixty, at the very peak of his teaching career. The comments he makes on the key concepts of wisdom, emptiness, mind, and others strike at themes at the very center of Buddhist experience. He delivers them in his inimitable style, directly from the source, with a vehemence that is designed

---

*In the final verse (page 87), Hakuin states the work was completed, and being printed, in 1744. As no copy of that printing is known to exist, there is no way of knowing whether that text was identical to the present one or not. It may represent an earlier version.

to dislodge assumptions and hardened preconceptions in the minds of students and to free them to find deeper self-understanding in the profound but highly abstract series of negations the sutra offers up to them.

Like the thirty or so other works that make up the *prajna,* or Wisdom, family of sutras, the teaching in the *Heart Sutra* focuses on the fundamental Buddhist doctrine of *shunyata* or emptiness. Although one of the briefest works in the Buddhist canon, the sutra is thought to embody within its two hundred and seventy Chinese characters—less than a page of text—the heart or essence of the Wisdom philosophy that is developed with great richness and resonance in such kindred sutras as the *Large Prajnaparamita Sutra,* an enormous work that amplifies the wisdom theme for fully six hundred volumes.

Through the centuries the *Heart Sutra* has been the most popular and widely used religious text in all East Asia. It is chanted on virtually every occasion in the Zen school and in most other Buddhist sects as well. There are few Buddhist followers unable to recite it by heart.

The teaching of the sutra is preached by the Bodhisattva Free and Unrestricted Seeing (Kanjizai in Japanese). This Bodhisattva, who is one of the most popular figures in the Mahayana Buddhist pantheon, is perhaps better known to Westerners by the Sanskrit name Avalokiteshvara, or the Chinese name Kuanyin. The Bodhisattva preaches at the request of Shariputra, who is reputed to be the wisest of the Buddha's disciples. Shariputra represents the teachings of the sage or Arhat, the ideal Buddhist disciple of the older "Small Vehicle" or Hinayana tradition that arose after the death of the Buddha and flourished prior to the appearance of the Mahayana teaching.

In setting forth the essentials of the *prajnaparamita,* the "perfection of wisdom," the Bodhisattva reveals to Shariputra how wisdom is achieved and the "other shore" of nirvana is reached through a process of negation in the course of which all existence and all assertions about existence, including the classic tenets of Buddhism, are shown to be empty and void of substance.

The *Heart Sutra* was probably composed in India about fifteen hundred years ago and was translated not long after that into Chinese. Since that time it has been explained and elucidated countless times. Commentaries in Japan alone run well into the hundreds, ranging from sophisticated expositions of Buddhist philosophy to simple religious tracts for the faithful. Generally, though, they all attempt to spell out the sutra's terse assertions along more or less rational lines. Primary appeal is to the intellect. Even those by monks with the most hardnosed reputations seem somehow conventional and well-mannered, more Buddhist than Zen, compared with the incisiveness and radical, shake-all attitude Hakuin brings to the text.

This quality, coupled with the vivid, paradoxical style characterizing Hakuin's half-joking—but totally serious— comments has earned the work its reputation as one of the classics of Japanese Zen. Since the first printed edition appeared in the mid-eighteenth century it has been a standard text in monasteries, where teachers use it in conjunction with Zen *teishō,* or lectures, to increase its effectiveness as a practical aid to training.

Hakuin's own title for the work, *Dokugo shingyō,* translates into English as "Poison Words for the Heart." The practice of attaching caustic, stinging comments in prose and verse to the words and phrases of Buddhist sutras and other texts has been a tradition among Zen teachers at least since the Sung dynasty. It was then that the most famous examples of the genre—the *Blue Cliff Record* (Pi-yen lu) and the *Gateless Barrier* (Wu-men kuan)—were composed. In Japan, where the tradition of capping verses goes back almost as far, Hakuin is widely regarded as one of the greatest exponents of the art. The virulence of his poison has become proverbial among the followers of his school. One drop, it is said, even a single word, can be fatal, destroying the universe and everything in it. They are quick to explain, however, how it works as a powerful medicine, pumping spiritual life into the dead letters of the sutra so they will work for students instead of against them, and how the master always doled it out with loving hands, an act of deepest compassion. Hakuin knew from his own religious struggle that it is only through the experience of what Zen calls the "great death" that students can emerge into the great life that lies beyond.

Over the last century many prominent Rinzai Zen teachers have produced commentaries on the *Dokugo shingyō*. Their works elucidate the difficulties of Hakuin's text for new generations of Zen students who, owing to the sharp decline in Chinese studies, are no longer conversant with the traditional Chinese-style texts. I have listed below those that have been especially helpful to me in translating Hakuin's comments. They have made attemptable a task which otherwise I probably would not have even considered undertaking. The bulk of the annotation in the notes also has been gathered, freely and frequently, from their pages—a true compilation, in its Latin sense of *pillage*.

A translation of this kind offers great possibilities for

annotation. Working on the principle that whatever is said about Hakuin's meaning usually restricts it, and that the safest guide through Hakuin's commentary is Hakuin himself, I have tried to keep that kind of note to a minimum. I have been more concerned with identifying the numerous allusions and supplying background information for the anecdotal material in which the work abounds.

SOURCES

1. *Dokugo shingyō kanwa,* Kawajiri Hōgin, 1908
2. *Dokugo shingyō,* Sugawara Jiho, 1920
3. *Dokugo shingyō kōwa,* Gotō Zuigan, 1940
4. *Dokugo shingyō,* Shibayama Zenkei, 1958
5. *Dokugo shingyō kōwa,* Yamada Mumon, 1981

Zen Words for the Heart

written by HAKUIN EKAKU

edited by HUNGER AND COLD

revised by COLD AND HUNGER

Kannon Bodhisattva

*H*akuin's Opening Remarks on Capping Words and Verses

Blind old futzer down in a dark cave thick with a maze of vines and creepers. He comes back and sits stark naked in the weeds. Pity about poor Master Fu. He's going to lose all his lovely mansions. And don't say these words are cold and indifferent, that they have no taste. One bellyful eliminates hunger till the end of time.

> Casting a forest of thorns over the entire universe
> He enwraps in its tangles every monk on earth.
> I hope that you will find your way to deliverance
> And enjoy yourselves hawking inside a lotus thread.

NOTES

Besides setting forth Hakuin's basic Zen standpoint, these opening remarks on the "capping words" and verses allude to the way in which their "poison" works to help bring students to attainment of true wisdom or enlightenment.

The *blind old futzer* is a reference to the Bodhisattva, Free and Unrestricted Seeing (Kannon, Kanjizai), who preaches the sutra, but must also refer to Hakuin himself, as author of the capping words and verses.

The *maze of vines and creepers* refers to verbal complications and conceptual understanding. Unable to stand on their own, they envelop and constrict the true wisdom and prevent it from working freely. Beneath the hard words is suggested the proper role of the Bodhisattva, who leaves the naked suchness of his own enlightenment and, undisturbed by obstructing senses, preaches to beings in the world of relativity (*the weeds*). Of his blindness, the modern Rinzai master Sugawara Jiho says: "Not being blind, we see mountains, rivers, men and women, and other things, and think this gives us a kind of freedom, while it is in fact the cause of our unfreedom. . . . The great Buddhist teachers of the past are people who went forward to become blind men."

Poor *Master Fu* is Fu Tashih, celebrated layman of early Chinese Buddhism, who was regarded as an incarnation of Maitreya, Buddha of the future. In the *Flower Garland Sutra*, Maitreya is depicted as dwelling in the splendidly bejeweled palaces of enlightenment he created in the Tushita heaven. The wisdom expounded in this sutra, and at work in Hakuin's own comments, negates everything in the universe; nothing can escape, not the dwellings of sentient beings immured within their selfhood, not even Maitreya's enlightened universe.

Lotus threads, appearing when the lotus root is cut, are fine, stringlike filaments formed from the viscous substance that exudes from the severed surfaces.

*T*he Great Wisdom Perfection Heart Sutra
(Mahaprajnaparamita Hridaya Sutra)

Maha (Great)

Maha

The Chinese translated this "great." But what is it? Not a thing in all the universe you can compare it to. Most folks think it means large and vast. *Wrong! Wrong!* Even a Superior Man has a love of wealth, but he knows the proper way to get it. Bring me a *small* wisdom!

> A thousand million Sumerus in a dewdrop on a
>   hair,
> Three thousand worlds inside a foam-fleck on the
>   sea;
> A pair of young lads in the eye of a midge
> Play games with the world, they never cease.

NOTES

Here and in the next four sections Hakuin comments on the words in the sutra's title.

Even a Superior Man has a love of wealth, but he knows the proper way to get it. To the Superior Man (a Confucian term here signifying Bodhisattva), wisdom is the only true wealth.

Sumeru is the mountain said to stand at the center of the world. The *three thousand worlds* constitute the universe in its entirety.

The *midge* is the *chiao-ming,* an infinitesimally small insect whose universe is a follicle of hair in the eyebrow of a mosquito.

Prajna

They translated this "wisdom." All people have it. No one's excepted. It's faultlessly perfect in each one of us. He plays around making mud pies like this. When's he going to stop? You never see it until your fingers let go from the edge of the cliff. Why? Don't pare your nails at the foot of a lamp. You might get an inchworm to measure longs and shorts, but don't ask a snail to plow a rocky field.

> Ears like the dumb. Eyes like the blind.
> An empty sky losing itself to midnight.
> Even Shariputra didn't get a good look,
> The clubfoot Persian crossed at another ford.

NOTES

Don't pare your nails at the foot of a lamp. A popular Japanese saying that is explained in a rather bewildering variety of ways. It is said to have been a favorite of Hakuin's teacher Shōju Rōjin. Here it presumably cautions students against relaxing their efforts as they strive toward realization.

You might get an inchworm to measure longs and shorts. Granting an inchworm or "looper" is measuring lengths as it hunches along, a snail (with horns, somewhat resembling an ox) cannot plow a rocky field. Don't ask the impossible.

Shariputra was foremost in wisdom among the Buddha's followers. The *Heart Sutra* is preached at his request.

8

The clubfoot Persian crossed at another ford. As Kannon explains wisdom, wisdom itself is long gone.

Paramita

The Chinese for this means "reach the other shore." But where is that? He's digging himself into a hole to get at blue sky. Shrimps may wriggle and jump, but they can't escape the dipper. The place where the Treasure lies is near at hand. Take one more step! Master Hsieh sits in his boat wringing water from his fishing line. Even the clearest-eyed monk is secretly troubled.

> Is there a soul on earth who belongs on "this
> shore"?
> How sad to stand mistaken on a wave-lashed quay!
> Pursued with the roots to life unsevered, practice
> Remains a useless struggle, however long it lasts.

NOTES

The *paramitas* are the practices Bodhisattvas undertake to escape the suffering of "this shore" and reach the enlightened realm of Nirvana or Buddhahood on the "other shore." In fact the other shore *is* this shore, which one can only attain by grasping the Buddha-nature within.

Master Hsieh sits in his boat wringing water from his fishing line. Hsieh is the family name of the ninth-century Chinese monk Hsuansha Shihpei, who lived as a fisherman before entering religious life. The futility of his attempts to wring the water from his line suggests the Bodhisattvas' purposeless activity as they dedicate themselves to helping their fellow beings across to the other shore. Such dedication is only possible when dualities of catching and not catching, this shore and that shore, are transcended. In the face of such deep attainment, even the most enlightened monks cannot help feeling a sense of inadequacy.

Heart

For untold ages it didn't have a name. Then they blundered and gave it one. When it flies into your eyes, even gold dust will blind you. A Mani Gem is just another blemish on the Dharma. *What is it!* Most people only think they have the real thing, like the man who confused a saddle remnant for his father's jawbone. The reason those who search for the Way remain unaware of its reality is simply because from the first they accept all their discriminations as true. *Those* have been the very source of birth and death since the beginning of time, yet fools call them "the original man."

> Clearly it's ungettable within the Three Worlds.
> An empty sky swept clean away. Not a particle left.
> On the zazen seat, in the dead of night, cold as steel.
> Moonlight through a window, bright with shadows
> of the plum!

Clearly it's ungettable within the Three Worlds. The Three Worlds are those of past, present, and future. Hence never, not at any time.

Sutra

"Thus I have heard. The Buddha was once . . ." *Faugh!* Who wants to roll *that* open! Most people go fossicking for "red and yellow scripture scrolls inside piles of worthless trash. Just plucking another clove off the lily bulb.

> This is one sutra they didn't compile
> Inside that cave at Pippali.
> Kumarajiva had no words to translate it,
> Ananda himself couldn't get wind of it.
> At the north window, icy drafts whistle through
>   cracks,
> At the south pond, wild geese huddle in snowy
>   reeds.
> Above, the mountain moon is pinched thin with
>   cold,
> Freezing clouds threaten to plunge from the sky.
> Buddhas might descend to this world by the
>   thousands,
> They couldn't add or subtract one thing.

NOTES

Thus I have heard. The Buddha was once. A traditional opening for Buddhist sutras.

Just plucking a clove. The bulb of a lily is composed of a number of smaller bulbs or cloves and has no real core; it *is* the cloves that make it up. To seek Wisdom by reading sutras one after another, says Hakuin, is like picking cloves off a lily bulb, looking for its center.

Kumarajiva is the great Central Asian monk celebrated for his translations of Buddhist sutras into Chinese, one of which is a widely used translation of the *Heart Sutra*.

Ananda is a disciple of the Buddha who is reputed to have heard and memorized all the preachings the Buddha made during his lifetime. He played an important role in the compilation of the first collection of sutras, said to have taken place inside the Pippali cave in central India.

*T*he Bodhisattva Free and Unrestricted
Seeing practices the deep wisdom paramita.
At that time he clearly sees all five skandhas
are empty and is delivered from all distress
and suffering.

Kannon

Bodhisattva

A provisional name, that's all it is. It helps set him apart from the Shravakas and the Solitary Buddhas. From full-fledged Buddhas as well. He's on the road but hasn't budged from home. He's away from home all the time, but he's never on the road. I'm going to snatch the practice of the Four Universal Vows from you. The very thing to make you Superior Men, able all eight ways.

> He transcends the formless nest of his personal
>   emptiness,
> Enters trouble-tossed seas in the great karmic ocean.
> Homage to the Great Merciful One who takes on
>   our suffering
> In a hundred million forms over boundless space
>   and time.

NOTES

For Hakuin, *Shravaka*s and *Solitary Buddhas,* who seek enlightenment for themselves but make no effort to teach others, represent a type of practice he regards as incomplete and inferior to that of the Mahayana Bodhisattva, who strives toward Buddhahood but out of compassion assists others to enlightenment as well.

Bodhisattvas manifest themselves in an infinite variety of forms in response to the needs of suffering beings, yet they remain always at home in the timeless realm of emptiness. This mode of being is reflected in the *Four Universal (Bodhisattva) Vows:* "Sentient beings are numberless, I vow to save them; the deluding passions are inexhaustible, I vow to destroy them; the Dharma gates are manifold, I vow to know them; the Buddha Way is supreme, I vow to master it."

The very thing to make you Superior Men, able all eight ways. In a Confucian setting this would refer to the eight Confucian virtues: benevolence, propriety, filiality, and so on. While the meaning of *able all eight ways* is uncertain in this context, the point of the statement as a whole seems to be that a Bodhisattva is not fully fledged until his Bodhisattvahood is transcended as well.

Free and Unrestricted Seeing (Kanjizai)

Why, it's the Bodhisattva of Butuoyan! The Great Fellow supplied to each and every person. Nowhere on earth can you find a single unfree soul. You cough. You spit. You move your arms. You don't get others to help you. Who clapped chains on you? Who's holding you back? Lift up your left hand—you may just scratch a Buddha's neck. Raise your right hand—when will you be able to avoid touching a dog snout?

> Fingers clasp, feet walk on, without help from
>   others,
> As thoughts and emotions pile up great stocks of
>   Wrong;
> But cast out pro and con, all your likes and dislikes,
> I'll confirm you as Kanjizai right where you stand.

NOTES

The sutra proper begins with the Bodhisattva entering deep meditation (*samadhi*) prior to preaching.

Kanjizai—Avalokitesvara in Sanskrit; Kuanyin in Chinese—stands as the embodiment of wisdom and compassion, the basic forces that impel all Bodhisattvas. In Japan he (or she) is more commonly known by the name *Kanzeon* (short form *Kannon*). Kanjizai, meaning "free and unrestricted seeing," represents the student or religious seeker striving for the highest level of wisdom; Kanzeon, "perceiver of the sounds of the world's [suffering]," represents the role of compassionate teacher, one who has postponed final attainment in order to teach others, vowing never to rest until the last being has also crossed the sea of suffering to the other shore of enlightenment.

Butuoyan, or Potalaka, is the original home or pure land of the Bodhisattva.

Practices

What's he prattling about now? Making waves. Stirring up trouble. It's sleeping at night. Moving around during the day. Pissing and passing excrement. Clouds moving, streams flowing, leaves falling, flowers scattering. But hesitate or stop to think and hell rears up in all its hellish forms. Yes, practice is like that all right, but until you penetrate by the cold sweat of your brow and see it for yourself, there's trouble in store for you, and plenty of it!

How about when you move your hands and feet?
Eating when you're hungry? Drinking when
    you're dry?
But if even a flicker of thought intervenes
You're killing Chaos to provide him with eyes.

NOTES

You're killing Chaos to provide him with eyes. This is a reference to a story in the *Chuang Tzu*. The gods, having finished creating a new world, decided to show their appreciation to Chaos, whose self-effacing help had been essential to their work, by supplying him with the same senses they themselves enjoyed. They bored holes in him to give him the sense of sight, but as they were congratulating themselves on the splendid results, Chaos died. Chaos alludes to what is prior to discrimination.

The Deep Wisdom Paramita

Bah! Gouging out healthy flesh, creating an open wound. Queer thing, this "wisdom" of his. What's it like? Deep? Shallow? Like river water, perhaps? Tell me about wisdom with deeps and shallows. Mistaken identity, I'm afraid. He's confusing a pheasant for a phoenix.

    Annulling form in the quest for emptiness is called
      shallow;

Seeing emptiness in the fullness of form is called
  deep.
He prattles about wisdom with form and emptiness
  in his clutches,
Like a lame tortoise in a glass jug clumping after a
  flying bird.

NOTES

Confusing a pheasant for a phoenix. This is based on an old
Chinese tale. The king of Ch'u was a great bird lover who
filled his palaces with feathered creatures of every kind.
An enterprising merchant hoping to gain his favor went to
Mount Tan where the phoenix was said to nest and
searched high and low for the mythical bird. As he was
about to give up and return home, he met a man carrying
a strange-looking fowl. It was actually a pheasant, but the
man told him it was one of the famous phoenix from
Mount Tan, so the merchant bought it and took it to the
king. The king thought it a rather poor-looking phoenix,
but it did have a long tail like a phoenix, and since a phoenix was said to be an auspicious bird, he accepted it with
great pleasure.

At That Time

He's done it again. Scraping out another chunk of per-
fectly good flesh. It's before all the infinite *kalpas* in the
past. Beyond all those to come. The marvelous Haircutter

Time

Blade gleams coldly in its box with a wonderful vibrant radiance. A pearl luminous in its setting brought forth in the blackness of night.

> Yesterday morning we swept out the soot of the old year,
> Tonight we pound rice for the New Year goodies;
> There's a pine tree with roots, oranges with green leaves,
> I put on a fresh new robe to await the coming guests.

NOTES

The *Haircutter Blade,* so sharp as to sever a hair blown against it, is a metaphor for the mind of wisdom.

The lecture meeting at which Hakuin delivered these comments on the *Heart Sutra* was held during the winter months. His verse expresses the essential oneness of time and being in the ordinary activities of temple life.

A *kalpa* is an immeasurably long period of time; an aeon.

He Clearly Sees

An invincible Diamond Eye, free of even the finest dust. Still, you don't go blinking it open over a bed of flying lime dust. Where does this "seeing" take place anyway?

The entire earth is the eye of a Buddhist monk. It's all exactly as Hsuansha said . . .

> A midge works a mill in the eye of a mite,
> A germ spins a web inside a nit's ear;
> Tushita heaven, the human world, the floors of hell,
> Stark clear as a mango in the palm of the hand.

NOTES

Where does this "seeing" take place anyway? Seeing presumes a seer and something seen, but no such duality exists in the deep wisdom paramita, where, as a well-known Zen saying asserts, "The entire universe is the eye of a Buddhist monk."

It's all exactly as Hsuansha said. The T'ang monk Hsuansha appeared earlier in the commentary. It is impossible to determine which, if any, of Hsuansha's sayings Hakuin has in mind here. Shibayama Zenkei, a modern Rinzai teacher, cites the Sung master Tahui, who in praising Hsuansha's utterances said that they possessed "a meaningless meaning."

All Five Skandhas Are Empty

The tail on the sacred tortoise sweeps all her tracks clear. But how can the tail avoid leaving traces of its own? Forms are like the towering Iron Hoop Mountains. Sensation and perception like the trenchant Diamond Sword. Conception and consciousness like the gem that fulfills the heart's desires. But you must realize how far there is to go. Before you know it darkness overtakes you once again.

> You see another's five and you think that's you,
> You cling to them with personal pride or shame;
> It's like the bubbles that form on the surface of
>   waves
> Like lightning bolts streaking across the sky.

NOTES

The *five skandhas*, or aggregates—form, perception, conception, volition, and consciousness—are the component elements of all sentient being.

But how can the tail avoid leaving traces of its own? After having said "All things are empty," the words "all things are empty" still remain.

The Iron Hoop Mountains circle the outer limits of the world. Like David Copperfield, Hakuin "sees nothing but makes it everything." Emptiness is far from being mere vacuity. Forms (one of the *skandhas*) have a presence as undeniable as mountains; the functions of the mind (the other four *skandhas*) work like an invincible diamond sword, annihilating illusion, and like the fabulous Mani Gem, fulfilling every wish. To grasp the true meaning of the *skandhas'* emptiness in this way takes years of rigorous training, and human life is all too brief.

Is Delivered from All Distress and Suffering

That shadow in the guest's cup never was a snake. How clear, in a dream, the three worlds are. When you wake, all is empty, all the myriad worlds are Mu.

> The ogre outside shoves the door,
> The ogre inside holds it fast.
> Dripping sweat from head to tail
> Battling for their very lives,
> They keep it up throughout the night
> Until at last when the dawn appears
> Their laughter fills the early light—
> They were friends from the first.

NOTES

That shadow in the guest's cup never was a snake. This is an allusion to the story of Yueh, a Chinese official who, when he was appointed governor, invited a friend to help him celebrate. He gave the friend a large cup of wine, but when the friend took it up to drink he saw a snake wriggling on the surface of the wine. He closed his eyes and gulped it down, but then begged to be excused and rushed home. Thinking he had swallowed the snake, he became ill and took to bed. Upon learning what had happened, the governor invited him again. Setting a wine cup before his friend, he asked if the snake was still there. When the friend replied in the affirmative, Yueh pointed to a bow hanging on the wall, a reflection of which had been cast on the surface of the wine. We create illusions such as the five *skandhas*, which become the cause of our suffering.

The verse recasts a story by the Buddhist scholar Nagarjuna about a pair of fellow travelers who lost their way and became separated deep in the mountains. One of them wandered aimlessly until overtaken by darkness. He approached a small, lonely cottage and asked the householder for lodging. The householder refused, saying he was being haunted by night goblins, but the traveler persisted and was finally allowed to stay. After supper there was a sudden rattling at the door. The traveler ran to the door and held it fast. All night long the banging and clawing continued outside the door, and the traveler, just as tenaciously, held it secure. When daylight came, the traveler could see that the supposed goblin was the friend he had been separated from the previous day, who had also come to the cottage seeking shelter.

The *ogre inside* is the courageous and resolute heart of the practicer; the *ogre outside,* his illusions and desires. *Dawn* is the opening of enlightenment, when it is realized that illusions are no other than enlightenment.

Shariputra, form is no other than emptiness, emptiness no other than form. Form is emptiness, emptiness is form. And it is the same for sensation, perception, conception, and consciousness.

二法門
了如何是不
等各自說
維摩詰言我
王子為眾問
兩特文殊法

Vimalakirti

Shariputra

Phuh! What could a little pipsqueak of an Arhat with his measly fruits possibly have to offer? Around here, even Buddhas and Patriarchs beg for their lives. Where's he going to hide, with his "Hinayana face and Mahayana heart"? At Vimalakirti's, he couldn't even get his manhood back. Surely he can't have forgotten the way he sweated and squirmed?

> In the Deer Park his wisdom surpassed all the rest
> He startled Uncle Long Nails while still in the
>   womb
> He went to the Great Man in person, took down
>   his sutra
> Was Rahula's private tutor, the clever Mynah
>   Lady's kid.

NOTES

The preaching begins with an address to Shariputra, who requested the sutra.

With his Hinayana face and Mahayana heart? Shariputra, though a follower of the Hinayana or Small Vehicle tradition who lived prior to the appearance of the Mahayana teaching, already possessed the truth of that teaching in his heart. In the *Lotus Sutra* the Buddha predicts that in the future his disciples will surpass the stage of Arhatship and achieve Buddhahood.

In the *Vimalakirti Sutra,* when the layman Vimalakirti and the Bodhisattva Manjushri discuss the role of the Bodhisattva, Shariputra is present, along with a celestial maiden of Bodhisattvic powers. Shariputra is resentful that a woman should be there, thinking she will defile the gathering, and engages her in debate on the possibility of enlightenment for women. He intends to put her in her place but reveals instead his failure to transcend the distinction of sex. She transforms him into a celestial maiden and challenges him to change himself back into a man, which he is unable to do because of the attachments that remain in his mind.

Uncle Long Nails is the brother of Shariputra's mother. Returning home after long and diligent study in great centers of learning, he was surprised to discover that his sister, expecting a child, had become extremely intelligent and eloquent and could easily best him in argument. Remembering that a woman carrying a child of great wisdom was said to acquire that wisdom herself, he realized he would have to study much harder if he was avoid being overshadowed by his new nephew. From then on he even grudged the time to cut his fingernails, which grew to a very great length.

The *Great Man* is Kannon. *Rahula* is the son Shakyamuni fathered prior to his entrance into religious life; he was taught by Shariputra and later became one of the Buddha's disciples. The *Mynah Lady* is Shariputra's mother Shari (Shariputra means "son of Shari"), who received her name, meaning "mynah bird," because of her eloquence and piercing eyes.

Form Is No Other Than Emptiness, Emptiness No Other Than Form

A nice hot kettle of stew. He ruins it by dropping a couple of rat turds in. It's no good pushing delicacies at a man with a full belly. Striking aside waves to look for water when the waves *are* water.

> Forms don't hinder emptiness; emptiness is the
>   tissue of form.
> Emptiness isn't destruction of form; form is the
>   flesh of emptiness.
> Inside the Dharma gates where form and emptiness
>   are not-two
> A lame turtle with painted eyebrows stands in the
>   evening breeze.

NOTE

The two *rat turds* are form and emptiness.

Form Is Emptiness, Emptiness Is Form

Rubbish! A useless collection of junk. Don't be trying to teach apes to climb trees. These goods have been gathering dust on the shelves for two thousand years. Master Hsieh sits in his fishing boat wringing water from his line.

> A bush warbler pipes tentatively in the spring
>   breeze;

By the peach trees a thin mist hovers in the warm
    sun.
A group of young girls, "cicada heads and moth
    eyebrows,"
With blossom sprays, one over each brocade
    shoulder.

NOTES

*Master Hsieh sits in his fishing boat wringing water from his
line.* Earlier in the commentary Hakuin used this phrase to
describe the apparently useless effort Bodhisattvas exert as
they strive to lead others to enlightenment. Here he chides
Kanjizai for repeating these needless assertions about form
and emptiness.

The verse depicts the *forms* from the actual world, which
are, in themselves, no other than emptiness.

Cicada heads and moth eyebrows are stock descriptions of
female beauty.

And It Is the Same for Sensation, Perception, Conception, and Consciousness

Just look at him now—wallowing in the sow grass! If
you pass these strange apparitions without alarm, they
self-destruct. Snow Buddhas are terrible eyesores when the
sun comes out. You certainly won't see strange things like
this around my place.

Earth wind fire water are tracks left when a bird
    takes flight;
Forms sensation perception conception are sparks in
    the eye.
A stone woman works a shuttle, skinny elbows
    flying;
A mud cow barrels through the surf, baring her
    bicuspids.

NOTES

Earth wind fire water are the four great elements of the material world. The *sparks* are the spots that appear when you rub your eyes.

The final lines of the verse, exemplifying the principle that sensation, perception, conception, and consciousness are empty, caution against the error of falling into a passive state of "empty" emptiness. The twentieth-century Zen teacher Sugawara Jiho calls them "secret passwords that gain entry into the truth of 'all things are empty.' "

Shariputra, all things are empty appearances. They are not born, not destroyed, not stained, not pure; they do not increase or decrease. Therefore, in emptiness there is no form, no sensation, no perception, no conception, no consciousness; no eyes, ears, nose, tongue, body, mind; no form, sound, scent, taste, touch, dharmas; no realm of seeing, and so on to no realm of consciousness;

Impermanence

Shariputra, All Things Are Empty Appearances

It's like rubbing your eyes to make yourself see flowers in the air. If all things don't exist to begin with, what do we want with "empty appearances"? He is defecating and spraying pee all over a clean yard.

> The earth, its rivers and hills, are castles in the air;
> Heaven and hell are bogey bazaars atop the ocean waves.
> The "pure" land and "unpure" world are brushes of turtle hair,
> Nirvana and samsara, riding whips carved from rabbit horn.

NOTES

Flowers in the air, the spots seen by those with eye disease, can be made to appear by rubbing the eyes.

Turtle hair and *Rabbit horn,* are stock metaphors for that which does not exist and, by extension, false notions and delusions.

The *pure land* is the Buddhist paradise, or "other shore" of Nirvana; the *unpure world* is the realm of transmigratory births and deaths in which we live.

They Are Not Born, Not Destroyed, Not Stained, Not Pure; They Do Not Increase or Decrease

Real front-page stuff! But is that really the way it is? How did you hit on that part about everything being not born and not destroyed? You'd better not swindle us! An elbow doesn't bend outward.

> The little chaps in your eyes are awaiting their
> guests,
> The Valley Spirit isn't dead, she expects your call.
> No one gets dirty living in the world of men;
> Not a clean face in all the Buddhas' pure lands.
> Eighty thousand shares of Dharma, isn't that
> enough?
> Three thousand Buddhalands contained in next to
> nothing.
> It's no different from the pillow prince of Hantan,
> Or the tax collector of Nanke, raking in the levy.

NOTES

The *little chaps* are "eyebabies" reflected in the eye. Working freely and mindlessly, they show all things as they truly are. The *Valley Spirit* is the echo; though void of any fixed substance or self, it responds instantly when someone calls out. These two lines illustrate the true principle of *Not Born, Not Destroyed*.

Eighty thousand shares of Dharma. There are said to be eighty-four thousand Buddhist teachings, one for each of the eighty-four thousand passions.

It's no different from the pillow prince of Hantan. This is based on a Chinese folktale. A young man who left home for a career in the capital stopped at a place called Hantan and, while waiting for his lunch to cook, took a nap and dreamed he had passed through an illustrious career, culminating in an appointment as chief minister of state. When he awoke and saw the food still cooking on the fire, he realized life was an empty dream and returned home.

The tax collector of Nanke. This is also from a Chinese folktale. A man fell asleep under a locust tree and dreamed he was summoned to the court of a king and asked to govern the difficult province of Nanke. Under his rule the people became wealthy enough to pay him taxes and make him a rich man. One day a messenger arrived to tell him the kingdom was in danger and the capital must be moved, and asked him to return to his original home until he was needed again. He woke up in the midst of a great storm. He later found a deserted anthill in the trunk of the locust tree; the ants had all left before the storm had struck.

Therefore, in Emptiness

A regular jackal's den. A cave of shadowy ghosts. How many pilgrims have fallen in here? A deep black pit. The unutterable darkness of the grave. What a terrifying place!

> Over a hundred cold hungry monks, a phoenix
>   brotherhood,
> Spread their winter fans and offer New Year
>   greetings.

Bodhidharma

On the wall hangs a blue-eyed old man with a
    purple beard,
In a jar are fragrant flowers of the chaste plum.
Cold to muzzle even the warbler's bright clear
    voice,
Warmth rising to the Zen seats from red-hot coals,
There are presents of wild yams, in plaits of straw,
And for old men, sugared sweets, laid in their
    wrappers.

NOTES

The verse describes the New Year's scene at the small
rural temple where Hakuin resided. In the previous section
he warned against attaching to empty emptiness; now he
offers concrete descriptions of true emptiness.

The *blue-eyed old man* is Bodhidharma, founder of the
Zen school, whose picture is hung during the New Year
period.

The cold is still too severe for the *uguisu*, or bush warbler, whose familiar pipings herald the coming of spring.

In the Zen hall a brazier is set out for the guests who
will come to pay their respects. The *yams* and *sweets*, of
which Hakuin was inordinately fond, are presents sent by
members of the lay congregation.

There Is No Form, No Sensation, No Perception, No Conception, No Consciousness

Dreams and delusions. Blossoms in the air. Why bother grasping at *them?* Profit and loss, right and wrong —*just leave them be.* This scrupulousness of his only stirs up trouble. What's the good of making everything an empty void?

> A boundless unencumbered space, open, empty, still,
> Earth, its hills and rivers, are only names, nothing more.
> You can quarter the mind, lump all forms into one,
> They're still just echoes murmuring through empty ravines.

NOTES

You can quarter the mind, lump all forms into one. This is an allusion to the Buddhist classification of the self into five *skandhas*: sensation, perception, conception, and consciousness (representing the spiritual aspect), and form (representing the physical aspect).

No Eyes, Ears, Nose, Tongue, Body, Mind; No Form, Sound, Scent, Taste, Touch, Dharmas; No Realm of Seeing, and So On To No Realm of Consciousness

Well, I have eyes and ears. A nose, tongue, body and mind! Forms, sounds, smells, tastes, touch, and dharmas *do* exist! Beneath an empty autumn sky stretch endless wastes where no one goes. Who is that horseman riding from the west?

> When the six consciousnesses stir, six dusts arise;
> When the mind root is at rest, the six dusts rest as well.
> Roots, dusts, and consciousnesses, all eighteen realms,
> Are vast a bubble of foam on a shoreless sea.

NOTES

Beneath an empty autumn sky stretch endless wastes where no one goes. Who is that horseman riding from the west? These lines are by Wang Ch'angling, a Chinese poet of the eighth century. Using them to depict the realm of total emptiness and the marvelous activity of enlightenment that emerges from within it, Hakuin calls on students to affirm the sutra's negations for themselves.

The *six roots* (eyes, ears, nose, tongue, sense of touch, and faculty of mind), interact with the *six dusts* (shape and color, sound, odor, taste, touch, and mental objects or dharmas), giving rise to six consciousnesses (sight, hearing, smell, taste, touch, and mind), thereby manifesting the external world to us. The first five roots and consciousnesses function in conjunction with the sixth (mind or faculty of mind), their source. When the mind root remains quiet and unattached, the *six dusts* do not arise.

No ignorance, no end of ignorance, and so on to no old age and death, and no ending of old age and death; no pain, karma, extinction, Way; no wisdom, no attaining.

Bodhidharma

No Ignorance, No End of Ignorance, and So On To No Old Age and Death and No Ending of Old Age and Death

Pearls scattered through a veil of finest purple silk. Pearls packed inside a filthy beggar's bag—it takes real wisdom to know *those* are jewels. The water a cow drinks turns to cream; the water a snake drinks turns to poison. The quiet twelve-storied mansions where sages dwell are wrapped in perpetual five-colored clouds far beyond man's reach.

> Twelve causes are produced and twelve are
>   destroyed;
> Producers are ordinary beings, destroyers called
>   sages.
> Such is the world that the Solitary Buddha sees,
> The dust in his eyes spinning around in emptiness.
> Who can really see the dust floating in his eyes?
> O cherished Dharma wheel, great, perfect, round,
>   sudden!
> Make your way into its light, confirm the dust
>   yourselves,
> Break free of those mangy fox carcasses you wear!

NOTES

The sutra gives an abbreviated list of the twelve links of the chain of causation: ignorance, contact, consciousness, name and form, the sense organs, touch, feeling, desire, clinging, becoming, birth, and old age and death. The first, ignorance (literally, "no light"), is the cause of all the rest, and these are both causes and effects of one another in an endless, unbreakable chain. The chain of causation, while usually associated with the Solitary Buddha who wins enlightenment by contemplating it and exhausting ignorance and the other links in the chain, is also the fundamental conception of human existence, based on a relation of causal origination and karmic transmigration, for Buddhism as a whole. In the Mahayana tradition, when "no light" is replaced by "light" or wisdom, all the links of the chain become, as such, the wonderful workings of wisdom.

Pearls scattered through a veil of finest purple silk. Seen by the enlightened eye, all the links of the chain that the sutra negates are sights of such splendor that words are not adequate to describe them.

The quiet twelve-storied mansions where sages dwell are wrapped in perpetual five-colored clouds far beyond man's reach. The five-colored clouds are the five *skandhas* or components of life that make up the material and mental aspects of the self. The *twelve-storied mansions* allude to the twelve-linked chain of causation within the self, which the enlightened truly see and experience as an abode of tranquility and bliss.

Break free of those mangy fox carcasses you wear! This is an allusion to a remark attributed to the Buddha: "I'd rather you be transformed into a mangy old fox carcass than for you ever to accept the one-sided truths of the Shravaka and Solitary Buddha."

48

No Pain, Karma, Extinction, Way

Shining gems in the dawn light beyond the bamboo
blind. The fool goes at them with an upraised sword! The
salt in the seawater, the size in the paint. Egrets settling in
a field, a thousand flakes of snow! Yellow warblers in a
tree, the branches all in flower!

Four burning bullets, red to the core, put on
Straw sandals at midnight and rise beyond the
clouds.
The Four Truths (pain, karma, extinction, Way)
aren't
At the end or the beginning, aren't perfect or
sudden.
Kaundinya, Bhadrika, Kulika, and the others
Got their face gates burnt off before they knew it.
The Golden Sage wasn't netting shrimps in the
Deer Park,
He was secretly anticipating their Mahayana roots.

NOTES

Pain, karma, extinction, Way. These are Four Noble
Truths the Buddha used to explain the causes of suffering
and path of deliverance.

Shining gems in the dawn light beyond the bamboo blind. The
gems are the Four Noble Truths. Not knowing the priceless
worth of the Four Truths, ignorant people and those of
lesser attainment like Shravakas and Solitary Buddhas re-

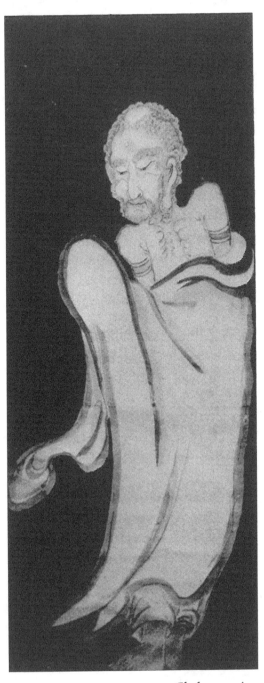

Shakyamuni

gard them as undesirable and attempt to do away with them.

Aren't at the end or the beginning, aren't perfect or sudden. This is a reference to a classification of the Buddha's teachings into five periods according to the order in which they were preached.

Kaundinya, Bhadrika, Kulika are three of the five ascetics who heard the Buddha's first sermon, in which he expounded the Four Noble Truths. They became his followers and later achieved the stage of arhatship.

The *Golden Sage* is the Buddha; the *shrimps* are Arhats who were present in the Deer Park when the Buddha first preached. Although it may appear that the Arhats were the object of the Buddha's teaching, the enlightened eye of the Bodhisattva can see that he was preaching the Mahayana Dharma all along. Shibayama Zenkei comments that it all depends on the person who is using the net: If his skill is great, he will come up not with shrimps but with people of great enlightenment.

No Wisdom, No Attaining

Setting up house in the grave again. So many misunderstand these words. A dead man peeping bug-eyed from a coffin. You can shout yourself hoarse at Prince Chang painted there on the paper, you won't get a peep out of him.

A black fire burning with a dark gemlike brillance
Drains vast heaven and earth of all their native color.

Mountains and rivers aren't seen in the mirror of
  mind;
A hundred million worlds agonizing, all for
  nothing.

NOTES

You can shout yourself hoarse at Prince Chang. This alludes
to a story about a prince who declared to his subjects that
after his death if they were ever in peril they only had to
go before his portrait and invoke his name, and he would
come to their aid. When the country was threatened by an
enemy army, people did as he had instructed, but to no
avail; the country soon fell to the invaders. Shibayama
Zenkei comments that even those who know the wonderful truth of *No Wisdom, No Attaining* cannot explain it in
words; it must be grasped for oneself.

A black fire burning with a dark gemlike brilliance. A black
fire, being almost indiscernible, burns and spreads with
great speed, consuming everything in its path.

*A*s he has nothing to attain, he is a Bodhisattva. Because he depends upon the wisdom paramita, his mind is unhindered; as his mind is unhindered, he knows no fear, is far beyond all delusive thought, and reaches final nirvana. Because all Buddhas of past, present, and future depend upon the wisdom paramita, they attain highest enlightenment.

Bodhisattva

As He Has Nothing to Attain,
He Is a Bodhisattva

Let go of it! The thief pleads innocence with the stolen goods in his hands.

Acting according to circumstances in response to sentient beings wherever they may be, he still never leaves the Bodhisattva seat. Unless you're clear about three and eight and nine, you'll have a lot to think about as you confront the world.

> Bodhisattva. Enlightened Person! Great Being!
> In Chinese, "Sentient Being of Great Heart."
> He enters the Three Ways, takes our suffering on
>   himself;
> Unbidden, he proceeds joyfully through every
>   realm;
> Vowing never to accept the meager fruits of partial
>   truth
> He pursues higher enlightenment while working to
>   save others.
> The vast void of boundless space might cease to be,
>   still he'd
> Urge his vow-wheel on forever to save the
>   ignorant multitudes.

NOTES

The thief pleads innocence with the stolen goods in his hands.
Hakuin says to let go of nonattainment too.

Unless you're clear about three and eight and nine . . . world.
While it seems generally agreed by the priests who comment on this phrase (taken from a Zen dialogue) that it defies intellectual understanding and can only be grasped through meditative insight, one of them offers this philological note: Three, eight, and nine add up to twenty; a Chinese character for the number twenty is sometimes used in place of the character *nien,* meaning thought or thinking.

The *Three Ways* are the unfavorable transmigratory realms of hell, hungry spirits, and animals.

Because He Depends Upon the Wisdom Paramita

What a choke-pear! He's gagging on it. If you catch sight of anything at all to depend upon, you must spit it out at once. I can endure the northern wastes of Yuchou, but the mildness of Chiangnan is sheer agony.

> Tell us you found greed and anger among the
>   Arhats, but don't
> Give us nonsense about Bodhisattvas depending
>   upon wisdom.
> If you see them depending upon anything at all,
> They're not "unhindered," they're shackled in
>   chains.
> Bodhisattvas and wisdom are essentially the same,
> Just like beads rolling on a tray—sudden, ready,
>   uninhibited.

He's neither worldly nor saintly, stupid nor wise.
A crying shame, when you draw a snake, to add
    a leg.

NOTE

A crying shame, when you draw a snake, to add a leg. The
"leg" is dependence upon wisdom.

His Mind Is Unhindered; As His Mind Is Unhindered, He Knows No Fear, Is Far Beyond All Delusive Thought

Nothing extraordinary about that. Supernatural power,
wondrous activity—just a matter of carrying fuel or draw-
ing water. Lifting my head, I see in the setting sun my old
home in the west.

Not mind or Buddha-nature or nirvana,
Neither Buddha, Patriarch, nor wisdom;
Ten worldfuls of ungraspable red-hot holeless
    hammer
Shattering empty space into boundless serenity.

Just parting his lips, he utters mighty lion roars,
Scaring the life from the foxes, rabbits, and badgers.
Wizardlike assuming the form of whatever is
    before him,
Changing freely according to the situation at hand;

Hearing Mother Li's left shoulder is ailing,
He cauterizes Granny Chang's right leg.
Delusive thoughts, fears, sorrows, and the rest
Are like a water drop cast down a bottomless gorge.

Dispatched to Ch'i, Ch'ih was wrapped in fine furs,
When Li died, he had a plain uncased coffin.
Shouts rouse the priest in the hermitage from his
     midday nap:
Village boys have broken the hedge and are stealing
     bamboo shoots.

NOTES

Each of the verse's four stanzas is keyed to one of the
four clauses in this passage of the sutra.

Ten worldfuls comprise the Dharma world in its entirety:
six realms of illusion (those of hell, hungry spirits, animals, fighting demons, human beings, and devas) and four
realms of enlightenment (those of the Shravakas, Solitary
Buddhas, Bodhisattvas, and Buddhas).

Hearing Mother Li's left shoulder is ailing refers to an old
Taoist story about Mother Li, a rich woman with a painful
growth on her left shoulder, who was taken by Granny
Chang to a Taoist healer. Knowing his patient disliked
moxacautery, he cured her by burning moxa on Granny
Chang's right leg.

Dispatched to Ch'i, Ch'ih was wrapped in fine furs. When
Confucius's disciple Ch'ih was dispatched on a mission,
Master Jan requested an allowance of grain to support

Ch'ih's mother. Confucius told him to give her a certain amount, but Jan actually gave her much more. When Confucius learned of it, he said, "When Ch'ih left on his mission, he drove sleek horses and was wrapped in fine furs. There is a saying, 'A Superior Man helps out the needy; he does not make the rich richer still' " (*Confucian Analects*).

When Li died he had a plain uncased coffin. After Yen Hui died his father begged Confucius for his carriage so he could sell it to buy an outer casing for his son's coffin. Confucius refused, telling him that when his own son Li had died, his coffin had had no outer casing, nor had he given up his carriage to buy one for him, because it was not proper that he walk on foot (*Confucian Analects*).

And Reaches Final Nirvana

This is the hole pilgrims all walk into. They fill it up year after year. He's gone off again to flit with the ghosts. It's worse than stinking socks! The upright men of our tribe are not like this: the father conceals for the sake of the son, the son for the sake of the father.

> The mind of birth-and-death in all beings
> Is as such the Buddhas' great nirvana.
> A wooden hen sits perched on a coffin warming an egg;
> A clay mare sniffs the breeze and canters back to the barn.

Nirvana

NOTES

The upright men of our tribe are not like this. Confucius, being told of a man in a neighboring country called Upright K'ung because he bore witness against his father when the latter made off with a sheep, said, "In my country, uprightness is somewhat different. The father shields the son, the son shields the father." Teaching students about "reaching final nirvana" can only harm them.

Because All Buddhas of Past, Present, and Future Depend Upon the Wisdom Paramita

Holding a good man down like this only cheapens him. The bare skin and bones are fine as they are. They have a natural elegance and grace. No need to lard them with paint and powder. There are no cold spots in a seething cauldron.

> Wisdom fathers forth the Buddhas of the three
>   worlds;
> The Buddhas of the three worlds all enact this
>   wisdom.
> Mutual inexhaustibility of host and guest . . .
>   *Onsoro!*
> Cranes screech in an old nest banged about by the
>   wind.

NOTES

Since a Buddha's wisdom is all encompassing, there should be nothing left over for him to depend upon.

Enlightenment

Mutual inexhaustibility of host and guest. This is an allusion to the endless interrelation that exists between all things. The Buddhas' enlightened eye sees each of those things as a manifestation of ultimate truth.

Onsoro is a dharani, or magic spell, said to contain mystic power. *Dharanis* are invoked in esoteric Buddhism to achieve union with Buddha. Here Hakuin uses it freely as a spontaneous (and untranslatable) affirmation of the ultimately inexpressible truth of wisdom. One commentator calls it the voice of the Buddhas of past, present, and future preaching and enacting wisdom.

They Attain Highest Enlightenment

Stop hammering spikes into empty space! A steer may give birth to a calf, but no Buddha was ever enlightened by relying on wisdom. Why? Because wisdom and enlightenment are essentially not-two. Besides, if he has anything left to get, he is no Buddha. It's like a blazing conflagration. If they draw too close, Buddhas and Patriarchs get burned to death, like everyone else.

> Otters will be catching fish in trees long before
> A Buddha is enlightened by relying upon
>   something;
> And declaring that a Buddha has something to
>   attain!
> Next he'll tell us of the Arhats' connubial bliss.

63

Next he'll tell us of the Arhats' connubial bliss. Arhats are celibate.

*K*now therefore that the wisdom paramita is the great mantra, the great and glorious mantra, the highest mantra, the supreme mantra, which is capable of removing all suffering. It is true. It is not false.

Kannon Bodhisattva

Know Therefore, That the Wisdom
Paramita Is the Great Mantra

Hauling water to sell beside a river. Don't drag those beat-up old lacquer bowls out here! Transcribe a word three times and a crow becomes a how, and then ends up a horse. He's trying to palm shoddy goods off on us again, like some shady little shopkeeper. When walking at night, don't tread on anything white; if it's not water, it's usually a stone.

> Cherish the great mantra of your own nature,
> It turns a hot iron ball into finest sweetest manna;
> Heaven, hell, and the world right here on earth—
> A snowflake disappearing into a glowing furnace.

NOTES

Don't drag those beat-up old lacquer bowls out here! At a certain mountain shrine in China, lacquer bowls that had been used for Taoist rites were cast into a rushing torrent. By the time they reached the village in the valley below, they were so damaged as to be utterly useless to the villagers.

Transcribe a word three times. The characters for "crow," "how," and "horse" are similar in form. When texts were copied and recopied by hand, scribes often mistook one character for another, sometimes changing the original meaning of a text completely. After all his explanations of wisdom, Kanjizai ends up with something altogether different from what he intended. He would be better off saying nothing.

When walking at night, don't tread on anything white. Moving in the pitch blackness of night (symbolizing emptiness), you are in a realm where "not one thing exists," so anything you might see is sure to be an illusion. Pay no attention to it, it can only harm you.

Cherish the great mantra of your own nature. When you grasp the wisdom within you through the experience known as *kenshō* ("seeing into your own nature"), all the afflicting passions and the suffering they cause transform into perfect freedom and bliss.

The Great and Glorious Mantra

Don't say "great and glorious mantra"! Break apart that rough, unshapen staff and the great earth's Indigenous Black stretches out on every side. Heaven and earth lose all their shapes and colors. Sun and moon swallow all their light. Black ink pouring into a black lacquer tub.

> Great and glorious mantra, round and perfect in
>   every being,
> Casts calm illumination over the hills and rivers of
>   the world.
> The vast barrier ocean of our age-old sins vanishes
> Like a foam bubble on the waves, like a spark in
>   the eye.

NOTES

Rough, unshapen staff is a metaphor for the self in its natural state. Hakuin tells students to forget about words such as "great and glorious mantra" and concentrate on the urgent business of realizing the great and glorious mantra (wisdom) in themselves. In so doing, the self and everything in the universe will be destroyed and they will find themselves in the total blackness of the undifferentiated realm of enlightenment—a place where not one thing exists.

The Highest Mantra

What about down around your toes? Bring me the *lowest* mantra! The sound of raindrops pattering over the fallen autumn leaves is sobering to the soul, but how can it compare to the splendid richness and intimacy of sunset clouds casting a warm glow over fields of yellowing grain?

The finest, the noblest, the first,
Enthralling even Shakya and Maitreya.
Though we all have it in us from birth,
Each has to die and be born again.

NOTE

The sound of raindrops . . . yellowing grain. The melancholy autumn scene depicted in the first of these two verses evokes the impermanence of life; the second evokes the true joy and splendor of life's fullness, which is only known by proceeding beyond the perception of impermanence and death (Emptiness) into the enlightened realm of ultimate Wisdom (the highest mantra). The final line of Hakuin's verse, "Each has to die and be born again," repeats this idea. In Zen literature the word "intimacy" often conveys an idea of oneness rather than closeness.

The Supreme Mantra

Gabble-gabble. All this talk makes two stakes appear. What happened to the single stake? Where is it? Who said, "There is no equal anywhere above, below, or in the four quarters"? *Break it apart! Smash it into little pieces!* How many times is that idle old gimlet Teyun going to climb down from the summit of Wonder Peak and hire a foolish old saint to help him fill the well with snow?

> Last winter the plum was bitter cold.
> A dash of rain. A burst of bloom!
> Its shadow is cast by the pale moonlight,
> Its subtle fragrance floats on the spring breeze.
> Yesterday you were only a snow-covered tree,
> Today your boughs are starred with blossoms!
> What cold and suffering have you weathered,
> Venerable queen of the flower realm?

NOTES

Teyun is a Bodhisattva who appears in the *Flower Garland Sutra* and later in the Zen literature of China and Japan.

With all his rough edges rounded off through years of constant work, Teyun appears to the unenlightened eye no more than an idle old man. But only someone of his deep compassion and commitment, who has reached the ineffable heights of enlightenment (*Wonder Peak*), is capable of returning to the world and engaging in "foolish," purposeless activity (filling the well with snow): devoting himself to the endless task of helping others to achieve enlightenment. Hakuin chides Kanjizai for attempting to reduce the wisdom *paramita* to the level of ordinary discrimination. As Hakuin's verse implies, it can only be grasped, and its marvelous results enjoyed, through years of arduous training.

Which Is Capable of Removing All Suffering

Picking a lily bulb apart to find a core. Shaving a square bamboo to make it round. Ripping threads from a Persian carpet. Nine times nine is now and always eighty-one. Nineteen and twenty-nine meet, but neither offers its hand.

> When you pass the test of mind and emptiness
> Your *skandhas* and elements become instant ash;
> Heavens and hells are broken-down old furniture;
> Buddha worlds and demon realms are blasted to
>   oblivion.
> A yellow bird chortles ecstatic strains of "White
>   Snow,"

A black turtle clambers up a lighthouse, sword in
    belt.
Any person who wants to join in their samadhi
Must prepare to pour rivers of white-beaded sweat.

NOTES

A *lily bulb* has no real center; it *is* the cloves that make
it up.

Kanjizai says nirvana is attained by removing suffering.
Hakuin says attempting to do that would be like throwing
out the baby with the bathwater, inasmuch as suffering
and nirvana are inseparable.

It Is True. It Is Not False

Liar! He's lying in his teeth right there. The arrow has
already flown the China coast. You rub elbows with him
all day long. How do you resemble him?

Master Yen of Ch'i bumped off three valiant men;
Szechwan Chiang subdued a brace of bold generals.
A counterfeit cockcrow gave fierce tigers the slip;
A sheep's head was dangled to peddle dog flesh.
A man pointed to a deer to see who'd submit;
A stepmother's bee dashed a father's fond hopes.
T'ao Chu led the beauty of Yueh to her death;
Chihsin surrendered himself to the ruler of Ch'u.

A man slept under a bridge, supped on charred
    wood;
A girl wept at a well for a clasp she'd thrown in.
A king's corpse got away in a load of ripe fish;
A father's chipped tooth gnawed off a son's ear.
Burning by day the log road along the cliffs,
Crossing by night at the Ch'ents'ang ford.
If your gaze penetrates the center of these,
A yard of cold steel glints like frost in its sheath.

NOTES

Each of the first fourteen lines of the verse alludes to
an episode from Chinese legend or history. Falsehood or
deception plays a central role in each episode, though in
most cases it is prompted by loyalty and devotion. Hakuin
is presumably referring to the often baffling and outra-
geous methods Zen teachers employ as they attempt to
push students across the threshold into enlightenment.

Master Yen was minister of the state of Ch'i. He con-
trived a plan to dispose of three faithful retainers whose
obstinacy and self-righteousness were the cause of constant
unrest. Calling them together, he presented them with two
peaches, but none would accept a peach if it meant denying
it to another. They deferred back and forth until finally, to
solve the dilemma, one of them committed suicide. The
others, not to be outdone, killed themselves as well.

Led by generals Chunghui and Tengai, the armies of Wei
launched a surprise attack on the kingdom of Shu (Szechwan) and, despite the valiant efforts of wily General

Chiang, subdued the Shu forces. The lord of Shu surrendered, and Chiang was captured as well. Recognizing Chiang's ability, Chunghui made him a counselor. When Tengai was ennobled for his services, Chiang, sensing Chunghui's deep resentment, persuaded him to slander his rival to the lord of Wei. The lord of Wei believed the charges and had Tengai imprisoned. Learning that Chunghui aspired to become ruler of Shu, Chiang incited him to insurrection. During ensuing battles between the lord of Wei and the rebel forces, Chiang killed Tengai in his prison cell, and later both he and Chunghui perished in the losing rebel cause. Though unable to defeat Wei as commander of the Shu forces, Chiang thus brought about the deaths of its two valiant generals.

For its aggressive policies, Ch'in was feared by its neighbors as a land of *fierce tigers*. The Ch'in emperor, after inviting the wise and courageous Meng Ch'angchun to serve at his court, decided he could not trust him, and would have had him executed had not Meng bribed the king's favorite to intercede on his behalf with the promise of the gift of a precious robe of white fox. Meng had presented the robe to the king on his arrival and was now obliged to steal it back to present it to the lady. Allowed to leave, Meng set out immediately before the theft could be discovered, reaching the border in the middle of the night, with the king's men hard on his heels. The barrier would not open until first cockcrow, so one of Meng's followers good at imitating birdcalls made a sound like a crowing cock, and Meng was able to escape to safety.

The fifth line refers to the powerful chief eunuch, Chaokao. Aware of the ill will some of his officials bore him,

Chao determined to test their loyalty. He presented a deer to the king and told him it was a horse. The king only laughed, but Chao insisted it was a horse and asked the officials present what they thought it was. Some agreed it was a horse, some remained silent, and a few said it was a deer. Chao promoted those who agreed with him and punished the others.

A stepmother, wanting her husband's favorite son out of the way, caught a large bee, pulled out its stinger, and placed the bee on the lapel of her robe, aware that her husband was watching from a distance. Seeing the bee, the son tried to brush it away. His father, thinking he was making improper advances toward his stepmother, reprimanded him angrily. The son's protestations of innocence were to no avail, and he was at last driven to suicide.

T'ao Chu (Chu of T'ao) is a sobriquet used by the famous minister Fanli. When Yueh was defeated by the lord of Wu, the Yueh forces were captured and put to death. The lord of Yueh begged for clemency, and despite warnings from advisers that he might later prove dangerous, the lord of Wu spared his life. The lord of Yueh was finally able to convince the lord of Wu of his fealty and was allowed to return to his own country, where he faithfully served the Wu interests and sent frequent offerings of tribute. The lord of Wu, his mind at rest, surrendered himself to a life of decadence. He asked Yueh to send him fifty beautiful maidens for his seraglio, and among them was Hsishih (the lady of Yueh), one of the celebrated beauties of Chinese history. The lord of Wu gave all his time to Hsishih, neglecting the government, which fell into decay. T'ao Chu, a faithful retainer of Yueh, then convinced the lord of Yueh that the time was ripe to avenge his earlier defeat. The Yueh forces marched and defeated Wu handily. The lord of Yueh took Hsishih as his concubine, disregarding the examples T'ao Chu recited to him of beautiful women who had been the ruin of a country. On their way back to Yueh, at a spot called Stone Lake, T'ao Chu put Hsishih in a boat and, taking her to the middle of the lake, explained that he would have to kill her for the sake of the country. Before he could, she flung herself into the water and drowned.

When the first Han emperor was besieged by the forces of Ch'u and had no hope of escape, a captain in his army named Chihsin told the king of Ch'u that his lord had decided to surrender and would proceed to the Ch'u headquarters through the eastern gates of the city. The soldiers of Ch'u gathered at the gates to catch sight of the emperor, but Chihsin took his place in a covered palanquin, allowing him to escape from the western gates. When the Ch'u king discovered the ruse, he had Chihsin roasted on a burning pyre.

The man who slept under a bridge was Yujang. He served as a vassal of Fan Chunghang, but he was not highly esteemed by his master, so when Fan was overthrown by Chihpo, Yujang offered Chihpo his services. Chihpo took a liking to him and Yujang became a trusted retainer. When Chihpo was killed by Hsiangtzu, ruler of Chao, Yujang tried again and again, without success, to avenge his death. Finally, swallowing charcoal and daubing himself with lacquer to disguise himself as a leper, he took up residence with other outcasts under a bridge and waited for the day when Hsiangtzu would pass over it. But when Hsiangtzu finally did come, his horse sensed Yujang's presence as it approached the bridge and refused to cross. Yu, discovered lying in wait, was apprehended. Hsiangtzu asked him why, having served the murderer of his first master, he was now so strongly bent on revenge. Yujang replied that while his first master had treated him like an ordinary man, Chihpo had always treated him with honor, and he wanted to requite him in kind. He begged Hsiangtzu for a piece of his clothing so that he could fulfill his vow before he was executed. Upon being given Hsiangtzu's coat, Yujang thrust into it three times with his sword, saying, "I can report this to Chihpo when I meet him in the next world." He then fell on his sword and died.

Houpai, a famous thief, saw a young girl weeping sadly beside a well as he was making off with an armful of valuables and stopped to ask what was wrong. She told him she had dropped a precious hairclasp into the well and was certain to be punished when she returned home. Feeling sorry for her, Houpai stripped off his clothes and climbed down after the clasp. But while Houpai was down the well, the girl, who was really Houhei, a famous thief in her own right, made off with the booty and Houpai's clothes as well.

Chaokao, the tyrannical minister who appeared before in the story about the horse and the deer, was accompanying the king of Ch'in on a hunting excursion far from the capital when the king suddenly died. Wanting to control selection of the king's successor, Chaokao kept the death a secret and took the king's body back to the capital in a palanquin as if he were alive. Afraid the smell of the decaying corpse might be noticed on the long journey, he had a large quantity of dried fish placed around the body to disguise the smell. His strategy worked, and the new king appointed him chief minister.

An eldest son in the west of China struck his father and broke two of his teeth. The father, incensed at this unfilial act, decided to prosecute him. The penalty, if convicted, was death. The son sought the advice of a clever acquaintance who, after a moment's thought, suddenly bit the son on the ear. He told him that when he was called before the magistrate and asked to explain his action, he should say his father had broken his teeth by biting the son's ear in a fit of rage. Using this ploy, the son escaped the executioner's block. On the way home, however, he was struck dead by a bolt of lightning.

The next two lines (*Burning by day* and *crossing by night*) refer to intrigue at the beginning of the Han dynasty. Hsiangyu, after leading a revolt against the lord of Ch'in, emerged as the most powerful force in the country. He proclaimed himself king of Western Ch'u and appointed Liupang ruler of the Han. Aware that Liupang had great ambitions of his own, and feeling uneasy having him near, Hsiangyu sent him to the land of Shu in the remote western region. Just in case, he continued to keep his troops battle ready. Changliang, a retainer of Hsiangyu who was secretly working for Liupang, assured Hsiangyu that Liupang no longer presented a threat. He advised him to make doubly sure by having the plank road over which Liupang would have to pass were he to attack burned and rendered impassable. With his rival effectively bottled within the mountainous borders of Shu, Hsiangyu finally felt secure. Changliang then sent word to Liupang that the time for attack was at hand. Liupang, using a secret road that crossed the river at a place called Ch'ents'ang, destroyed Hsiangyu's armies and went on to establish the Han empire.

Therefore, I preach the wisdom paramita mantra, preach this mantra and say:

GATE GATE PARAGATE

PARASAMGATE BODHI SVAHA!

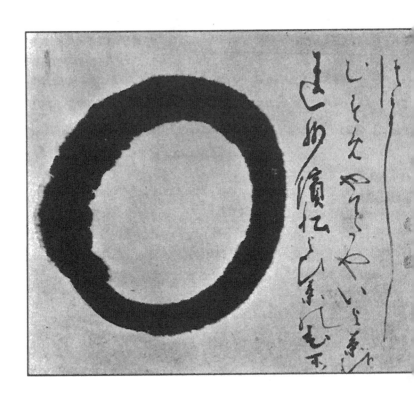

Therefore, I Preach the Wisdom Paramita Mantra

Well, what have you been doing up till now! It's like having a teetotaler forcing wine down your throat. You don't get the real taste of the drink swilling cup after cup. Unable to return for ten full years, you forget the way you came.

> He preached it once, now he trots it out again!
> Snowdrifts accumulating over accumulated
>   snowdrifts.
> There isn't any place you can hide and escape it,
> So who's the wine for? We're all drunk to the gills.

NOTES

Unable to return for ten full years, you forget the way you came. This line is a verse from the poems of Hanshan, or Cold Mountain. After years of practice, enlightenment deepens until it becomes free of any trace or odor of enlightenment. One commentator offers more detail: *Ten years* stands for the ten worlds, or realms, of living beings (the universe); to detach oneself from these realms is to become a Buddha, who is no longer affected by the karmic influences of the ten worlds. This is the real meaning of the wisdom *paramita*.

Preach This Mantra and Say:

He's still at it! Over and over! What about woodcutters' songs? Fishermen's chanteys? Where do they come in?

What about warbling thrushes and twittering swallows?
When you enter the water, don't be culling bubbles from
the waves.

These weed-choked fields in seven-word furrows,
These castles of verbiage in lines of five,
Weren't meant for the eyes of flinty old priests,
I wrote for you monks, cold and hungry in your
    huts;
For unless you find the Way, and can transform
    yourselves,
You stay trapped and entangled in a bottomless pit.
And don't try to tell me my poems are too hard,
Face it: the problem is your own eyeless state.
When you come to a word you don't understand,
    quick
Bite it at once! Chew it right to the pith!
Once you're soaked to the bone in death's cold
    sweat
All the koans Zen has are yanked up, root and stem
With toil and trouble, I too once glimpsed the edge
Smashed the Scale that weighs with a blind arm.
Once that tool of unknowing is shattered for good,
You fill with the fierceness and courage of lions.
Zen is blessed with the power to bring this about,
Why not use it and bore on to perfect integrity?
People these days turn from Zen as if it were dirt,
Who is there to carry on the life-thread of wisdom
I'm not just an old man who likes writing poems,
I want to inspire true seekers, wherever they are.

The superior will know at once where the arrow
  flies,
Others will just carp about my rhythm and rhyme.

Ssuma of the Sung was a true prince among men,
What a shame eyes of such worth remained
  unopened.
Whenever he read difficult, hard-to-pass koans
He said they were riddles made to vex young
  monks;
For gravest crimes a person must always be
  repentant,
Surely slander of the Dharma is no minor offense!
Crowds of these miscreants are at large in the world,
The Zen landscape has a barrenness beyond belief.
Once you've grasped the mind of the Buddha-
  Patriarchs
How could you possibly remain blind to their
  words?
To determine how authentic your own attainment
  is,
The words of the Patriarchs are like bright mirrors.
Zen practice these days is all cocksure and shallow,
They follow others' words, or fancies of their own.
When hearsay and book learning satisfy your needs,
The patriarchal gardens are still a million miles
  away.
So I beseech you great men, forget your own
  welfare!
Make the five-petaled Zen flower blossom once
  more!

NOTES

What about woodcutters' songs? Fishermen's chanteys? To the enlightened eye all things are preaching the wonderful wisdom mantra. In making distinctions Kanjizai only creates the cause of illusion.

The Scale that weighs with a blind arm is a scale with no markings or calibrations on the balance arm. It is a symbol for the mind or self, the fundamental source of ignorance, which is incapable of accurate measurement yet which the unenlightened make the basis of their discriminations. Here, it may refer to the mind that has broken through into the undifferentiated realm of emptiness but that now must also transcend that realm as well.

Ssuma of the Sung was a true prince among men. The famous eleventh-century Confucian scholar Ssuma Kuang was not actually anti-Buddhist. Hakuin criticizes him for misleading students by misunderstanding or misrepresenting the Zen teaching in his writings.

The five-petaled Zen flower is a reference to the five schools that appeared during Zen's golden age in the T'ang dynasty.

GATE GATE PARAGATE

PARASAMGATE BODHI SVAHA!

To serve a Superior Man is easy. To please him, an impossible task. A shred of whirling mist sails together with a lone white gull; the autumn waters are a single color with the far autumn sky. A rainsquall sweeps the sky, from a hamlet in the south to a hamlet in the north. A new bride carries a box lunch to her mother-in-law in the fields. Grandchild is fed with morsels from grandfather's mouth.

It's now midwinter, the first year of Enkyō,
My students got together, had these words
Carved on wood (each character cost ten *mon*,
more than two thousand in all!), they wanted
To preserve these dream babblings of mine.
I have added this final verse for them,
A tribute of thanks for their kindness.

My verses finished, I clasp my hands in prayer:
Though empty space should cease, my vow will
     never end;
Any merit this praising of wisdom may bring me
     I transfer
To others, to turn them to the realm of suchness,
Trusting myself to the Buddhas of the three worlds,
To the Patriarchs and sages in all directions,
To every deva, naga, and demon guarding the Law,
And every god in the Land of the Mulberry Tree;
I pray that all the brethren living with me here,
Their resolve steadfast, their minds diamond-hard,
Will move with dispatch, break beyond the barrier,
And with the gem of the precepts ever round and
     bright
In mind, sweep clear the demons of illusion every
     one,
And benefit without rest the vast suffering
     multitudes.

Self-Portrait by Hakuin

NOTES

GATE GATE PARAGATE PARASAMGATE BODHI SVAHA! The sutra ends with this mantra, or mystic spell, well described by D. T. Suzuki as a spontaneous affirmation of enlightenment emerging from Kanjizai's inner being. The usual translation is "O Wisdom, gone, gone, gone to the other shore, landed at the other shore!" though Tenkei Denson, a seventeenth-century Sōtō teacher, points out that "any attempt to apply reason or logic here will only reduce the mantra to a dead and lifeless utterance."

To serve a Superior Man is easy. To please him, an impossible task. Hakuin applies this saying from the *Confucian Analects* to the Bodhisattva or Zen teacher who, because he treats people with compassion according to their capacities, is easy to serve, but who, because he is also completely impartial, is impossible to please unless you are in accord with the Way.

A shred of whirling mist sails together with a lone white gull; the autumn waters are a single color with the far autumn sky. Commentators seem to agree that Hakuin uses these lines from the T'ang poet Wang Po to express the relation this final esoteric mantra has to the exoteric portion of the sutra that Kannon has previously preached: they are different, but they are one, a relation in keeping with "logic" of the Wisdom sutras.

A rainsquall sweeps the sky, from a hamlet in the south to a hamlet in the north. A new bride carries a box lunch to her mother-in-law in the fields. Grandchild is fed with morsels from grandfather's mouth. This quotation from the Sung poet and Zen layman Huang Tingchien is used by Hakuin to express

Zen layman Huang Tingchien is used by Hakuin to express the marvelous everyday reality of the wisdom *paramita*. Sugawara Jiho calls it "the farthest reaches of Zen attainment, Hakuin's own wisdom *paramita* mantra."

The first year of Enkyō fell in 1744. Hakuin was sixty years old.

The Land of the Mulberry Tree is a poetical name for Japan.

The Text of the
Great Wisdom Perfection Heart Sutra

The Bodhisattva Free and Unrestricted Seeing practices the deep wisdom paramita. At that time he clearly sees all five skandhas are empty and is delivered from all distress and suffering.

"Shariputra, form is no other than emptiness, emptiness no other than form. Form is emptiness, emptiness is form. And it is the same for sensation, perception, conception, and consciousness. Shariputra, all things are empty appearances. They are not born, not destroyed, not stained, not pure; they do not increase or decrease. Therefore, in emptiness there is no form, no sensation, no perception, no conception, no consciousness; no eyes, ears, nose, tongue, body, mind; no form, sound, scent, taste, touch, dharmas; no realm of seeing, and so on to no realm of consciousness; no ignorance, no end of ignorance, and so on to no old age and death, and no ending of old age and death; no pain, karma, extinction, Way; no wisdom, no attaining. As he has nothing to attain, he is a Bodhisattva. Because he depends upon the wisdom paramita, his mind is unhindered; as his mind is unhindered, he knows no fear, is far beyond all delusive thought, and reaches final nirvana. Because all Buddhas of past, present, and future depend upon the wisdom paramita, they attain highest enlightenment. Know therefore that the wisdom paramita is the great mantra, the great and glorious mantra, the highest mantra, the supreme mantra, which is capable of removing all suffering. It is true. It is not false. Therefore, I preach the wisdom paramita mantra, preach this mantra and say: GATE GATE PARAGATE PARASAMGATE BODHI SVAHA!

Printed in the United States
by Baker & Taylor Publisher Services